SUNBUDDY FABLES

BOOK 3

Copyright © 2014 Rae Dornan
www.SunRaeProductions.com

All rights reserved.
For permission to reproduce parts of this book, please contact the author.

Cover and book design by Andrew Osta
www.AndrewOsta.com

First Printing: USA, September 2014
ISBN 978-0-9896218-5-4

CHARLIE
THE FAT CHEETAH

(Jo'burg, South Africa) 24-12-1993

CHARLIE THE FAT CHEETAH

1.

Charlie the fat cheetah
couldn't run,

Might seem funny,
for him it wasn't fun.

Others laughed,
on the social scene,

Shouting,
"You silly old has-been."

2.

Sad,
as he was sleek and fast,

A huge joke now,
always last.

"I'm done," he said,
"I'm losing weight.

No more partying,
I'm going straight."

3.

"You Charlie?"
others laughed and did cry.

"Yeah me," he said,
letting out a sigh.

"Right," he thought.
"First thing to do,

Is brighten up
and stop feeling blue."

4.

"But no aerobics classes,
over the hill,

Up and down trees,
makes me ill.

I'll run slowly,
on the elephant track.

Gradually strengthening
my aching back.

CHARLIE THE FAT CHEETAH

5.

"Animals I attack,
I completely miss.

I'm so obese,
I fell into a fat abyss.

I need to jump up
with four feet,

As I'll never catch prey,
never eat."

6.

"Even walking
puts me in a lather.

I'm tired,
how much farther?

I'll dream on it,
wake and rise,

So a lame Gazelle
will be my prize."

7.

Others
didn't want to know

A cheetah
so pathetically slow.

Puffing and panting
with no mate.

Embarrassing his species,
what a state!

8.

Drinking his fill,
fat belly on the ground,

Along crept a Lion,
making no sound.

He was onto Charlie,
before he could react.

In deep trouble now,
it was a chilling fact.

9.

"Well," purred Lion
"What's here?

You, defenceless
I smell your fear."

Charlie knew
he couldn't bluff,

Done in,
he'd had enough.

10.

"You talk
like I've committed a crime.

I've been ridiculed,
for the last time.

I'm so depressed,
fit to burst.

You wanna kill me?
Do your worst!"

11.

"But Lion,
I'm not about to skulk.

I'm nearly as big as you,
I carry bulk.

So bully boy,
let's get it on or go

I'm ready
for our gruesome show!"

12.

Lion uttered
not a single word,

Threatened by a cheetah,
absurd!

"Mmmm,
you could pack a blow.

You're brave too,
I'll let you go."

13.

Charlie walked off,
brave as can be.

A distance away,
he sat under a tree.

"I just fronted the biggest
African cat?

I'm alive
because I'm cuddly and fat!"

14.

His fitness
and confidence grew.

He knew exactly
what to do.

Regaining his speed,
his gift from birth

He was a cheetah,
fastest animal on Earth.

SAM THE GREAT WHITE SHARK

(Durban, South Africa) 19-1-1993

SAM THE GREAT WHITE SHARK

1.

A Great White shark,
is a sight to see,

They call the shots,
in the deep blue sea.

Swimming effortlessly,
an amazing sight,

Sam the shark,
you don't want to fight.

2.

"I'm bad,"
filtered through his brain,

Not too bright,
but he could dish out pain.

"My teeth,
chop anything up,

Big fish
or a seal pup."

3.

"Every creature's,
scared of me.

I'm the absolute ruler,
in the sea.

I like to see fear
in an eye,

Before they're devoured,
and die."

4.

"I was made,
to destroy, and eat,

I'm living perfection,
totally complete.

I'm 10 metres long,
not an ounce of fat.

Who do you know,
built like that?"

5.

"None
is the answer, I know.

There's nowhere,
I'm afraid to go.

I'm so tough,
I use the coral reef

To clean my lethal,
serrated teeth!"

6.

Sam was
a nasty piece of work,

Ocean creatures,
thought him a burk.

He chased others,
close to him,

He did this,
with a huge grin.

7.

"I've no competition
to defeat.

If I had 'em,
all would grovel at my feet."

Then he saw,
a hundred kilo tuna,

Thinking,
"He's mine, another loser."

8.

In a flash,
blood and guts were everywhere.

Sam devoured him,
without a care.

He exploded,
"I haven't eaten enough!

I liked the tuna,
though he tasted tough."

SAM THE GREAT WHITE SHARK

9.

A school of dolphins
heard the din,

One pointed to Sam,
with a flick of a fin.

"He's rotten,
totally unfair.

He needs lessons,
about being fair."

10.

"We all know,
he's got to eat.

He's a shark,
it's no mean feat

To catch others
who swim past.

It's not like
he was born to fast!"

11.

Another said,
"I'll entice him over here.

He'll think
the coral is safe and clear.

I'll swim though,
and then we'll see.

I know he'll come
chasing after me."

12.

Dolphin laughed
at the Great White,

Who sped after him,
ready to fight.

The mammal entered,
the narrow coral reef,

The Great White raged,
gnashing his teeth.

13.

Sam got caught,
he couldn't move,

Wedged tightly,
in an airtight groove.

He tried,
but he was tightly stuck in,

In the end,
he couldn't move a fin.

14.

"Well," said dolphin,
"How the mighty fall!"

All others sea creatures,
heard his call.

"So big Sam,
how do you feel

About missing
your next meal?"

15.

Sam said,
"You'll be my next dish!

I eat mammals,
as well as fish."

"Dream on," said dolphin,
"But you're not free.

You're trapped,
compliments of me."

16.

Finally Sam escaped
from the coral reef,

With floppy skin,
bone, and dirty teeth.

He lost confidence,
and loads of weight,

A skinny Great White,
a pathetic state.

SAM THE GREAT WHITE SHARK

17.

He was never big headed again,
that's true,

As he cruised silently,
through the endless blue.

His lesson:
with brawn you can't always win,

Against smart mammals,
especially, a dolphin.

THE GREEDY MOSQUITO

(Durban, South Africa) 19-1-1993

THE GREEDY MOSQUITO

1.

"I'm starving,"
said mozi to his mate,

"Are you certain
it's not late?"

"I am," said the other,
"Sure as I can be,

"That we only feed
when others can't see."

2.

"I want a blood fest
do my worst.

I'm hungry,
dying of thirst.

I fancy an appetizer,
a wee bite.

I can't wait
until tonight,"

3.

"Well go by yourself,
I'm staying put

I'm not leaving
till it's black as soot.

I know the rules
of our life's game

If you're squashed,
you're to blame."

4.

"You worry too much,
you do.

Sometimes,
you haven't a clue.

Just be sly,
don't land with a thud,

Then drink
the human's blood."

THE GREEDY MOSQUITO

5.

He took off,
looking for prey

At the beginning
of the new day.

A drunken man
snored on the ground,

He landed on his leg
without a sound.

6.

After gorging
he could hardly fly at all.

Full of blood,
he nearly did stall.

In the air,
the sun came up for the day,

He thought,
"My munchies are now at bay."

7.

Seeing his mate he said,
"I'm done.

You missed
all the fun.

Fortune favours
the brave.

That's me,
nobody's slave."

8.

Both fell asleep
as the day was bright.

Sunlight for mozis
a horrible sight.

They woke
 as the sun went down.

Arrogantly,
he spoke like a clown.

THE GREEDY MOSQUITO

9.

"I'm going out,
right now

To find
a big fat tasty cow.

Although humans
taste very nice,

The danger
adds a little bit of spice."

10.

His mate said,
"Go on your way.

I've more respect
for our prey.

One whack,
and it's all over,

No more goodies
and clover."

11.

He flew off
into the light,

Scanning the ground,
in full flight.

"I'll going in
for the kill!"

He dropped
for his liquid meal.

12.

He landed on a man's
exposed thigh,

Thinking,
"Perfect landing, first try."

He sucked blood
for all he was worth,

Expanding his quickly
growing girth.

13.

The man stood,
without a sound,

The fat mozi,
fell to the ground.

Unable to fly
in the light of day,

He was now exposed,
easy prey.

14.

Ants eat everything,
day or night.

Easier for them,
with victims in sight.

He didn't listen
to his wise mate,

Arrogance determined
his gruesome fate.

PETE THE PIRANHA

(Durban, South Africa) 20-01-1993

PETE THE PIRANHA

1.

Piranha fish
live in the Amazon,

There's no river
close to comparison.

Shoals live
in a confined space,

Eating
is like a hysterical race.

2.

Pete was down
this day,

Fed up,
in dismay.

"What's up?"
his mate did ask.

"Meal times," he said,
"Are such a task."

3.

"But it's always
 like that,

We share,
so none get fat."

"I know,
I've eyes that see,

I want something,
just for me."

4.

Phil smiled,
"What to do?"

Knowing Pete
felt blue.

"Hey Pete,
let's take off,

Let's go find
a bit of scoff."

PETE THE PIRANHA

5.

They swam off
to look about.

Pete's mind
was full of doubt.

Both took stock
of the situation,

Falling into
deep contemplation.

6.

Pete recovered first
"Look there!"

A fish alone,
who didn't seem to care.

Phil said,
"Something's not right,

He's hasn't taken off
in fright."

7.

"Strange,
wriggling like that!

He's big,
 yummy and fat."

"'He is," said Pete,
"I'm off!

I fancy,
a good scoff."

8.

Once there,
he took a huge bite,

Not believing,
such a huge might

Could lift him,
through the air,

Phil watched,
in total despair.

9.

Placed under
a fisherman's seat,

He looked at
both his feet.

Blinded by the sun
unable to breathe,

In a situation,
he couldn't believe.

10.

He was dying;
it was close now.

"I've got to get out,
but how?"

The man's ankle,
was in his sight,

For the second time,
he took a bite.

11.

The fisherman screamed,
crash!

Both fell in,
with a huge splash.

Pete guzzled water,
into each gill,

As oxygen had gone
for the kill.

12.

Phil bubbled,
sighs of relief,

Exhaling
from gaps in his teeth.

The man swam,
at his best,

Never having
so much zest.

13.

Pete said,
"That was close for me!

Breathing air
nearly ended me.

Forget being
an individual winner,

Ending up
as the fisherman's dinner."

14.

He hated being
in the sun,

"Lesson learnt,
I'm done.

I'm part
of a pirahna shaol.

My purpose
is a group soul."

CYRIL THE CROCODILE

(London, UK) 27-01-1994

CYRIL THE CROCODILE

1.

"How's it goin'?"
the croc said to his mate.

He scurried along
at an alarming rate.

"Can't stop Cyril,
I'm working out.

Getting fit
is what it's all about."

2.

"I know mate," said Cyril
with a grin,

His mate
looked like his twin

Both were young
and very small

There wasn't much of them
at all.

3.

The Northern Territories
are in the land of OZ

Cyril asked about this
mum said "Cos,

Crocs are happy,
in a humid clime.

In the swamps,
life is fine."

4.

"Oh,"
Cyril showed all his teeth,

Looking at mum,
with total belief.

He said,
"I'm a lucky young croc,

With your love,
and no nasty shock."

CYRIL THE CROCODILE

5.

"Exactly,
that's what I mean,

You don't even need
to stay clean.

But strengthen your legs,
by exercise

Build them up
into a bigger size."

6.

"Why mum?
What'll come close to you?

Any attack me,
I know what you'll do.

You'll gobble 'em up,
just for fun!

You rule
under the Ozzy sun."

7.

"Please,
just do as you're told.

I know you're brave
and bold.

There's reasons,
I tell you this.

Practise time,
don't miss."

8.

He followed instructions
by mum.

She was serious,
this wasn't fun.

He scurried about
at lightening speed,

Sweating and panting,
for whatever he'd need.

9.

Both crocs grumbled
a lot of the time.

Mum's acting
like they'd committed a crime.

Pushed to do
more and more,

They became
confused and unsure.

10.

Their ordeal
seemed to go on forever,

Always running
in the muggy weather.

Monsoon rains come
every year

Weather patterns
make the air clear.

11.

One day,
they cruised for a laugh,

Feeling good,
after a swim and a bath.

The heavens opened,
with torrential rain

When it hit them,
it caused pain.

12.

Still it poured
and didn't abate,

Bringing them closer
to their fate.

Tropical flash floods
suddenly appear,

Huge bodies of water,
are suddenly near.

13.

It created
a five metre river across,

Three metres deep,
impossible to cross.

Sweeping all,
incredibly fast,

Nothing
survives in its path.

14.

Both crocs,
heard it first,

Like a huge river,
whose banks had burst.

Both ran
towards higher ground,

Close to
the termite mound.

15.

On high ground,
they started to slide.

In big trouble now,
nowhere to hide.

They turned,
running the other way,

Their only chance,
back into the fray.

16.

Their training helped
not just a little bit,

As they had become
really very fit.

They made it to safety
with their last breath,

Avoiding the danger
and a watery death.

17.

They saved themselves
in the nick of time,

Fully understanding
the watery clime

Cyril said,
"Thank goodness we could run!

It saved our lives,
as we were done."

GERRY THE GIRAFFE

(London, UK) 14-02-1993

GERRY THE GIRAFFE

1.

High up,
Gerry surveyed the ground,

Looking for Lions,
prowling around.

You'd look too,
if that was your plight,

To stay alive,
by using your sight.

2.

He was only checking,
no more than that,

As most lions around
were healthy and fat.

Scanning is smart,
on the savannah plain,

You don't live long,
being thoughtless and vain.

3.

He always tried
to do right,

Vigilantly using
his sight

It's a cool thing
to do,

To scan,
under the sky blue.

4.

Living on a saltpan in Namibia
is so hot.

Having shade at midday,
is a crucial spot.

He looked over
the shimmering horizon,

Never wanting,
much surprising.

GERRY THE GIRAFFE

5.

It was a typical African scene
over there.

Lions were top predator
with a neutral stare.

Giraffes
can be on the lion's dinner plate

They try to catch them,
laying in wait.

6.

Gerry took this in his huge stride,
as you do.

All have to accept fate,
including me and you.

But sometimes it's hard
to be cool and serene,

Knowing lions
want to pick your bones clean.

7.

Giraffes only want
to roam about,

Having a peaceful life,
no doubt.

They want to eat leaves,
between each thorn,

From acacia trees,
since they were born.

8.

Gerry was looking
for other giraffes.

He wanted company
and fancied a laugh.

It's safer too,
being in a group and together.

Solitary prey are hunted
in any weather.

9.

At tree level,
he's looking for his own.

Close by he spotted a head,
fully grown.

His mate Gill,
had the longest neck of all,

Longer that Gerry's,
ridiculously tall.

10.

Gerry froze,
as he saw for himself

A praid of lions
were moving with stealth.

The giraffes were four female
and three male.

He had to react,
he just couldn't fail.

11.

He was stunned,
frozen with fear.

His mind foggy,
nothing was clear.

"I'll have to sacrifice myself,
that's all,

To save the others,
and my mate so tall."

12.

Close by were a herd of elephants,
all black,

"That's it,
I'll get them to attack!"

He ran between the lions and tuskers,
in the middle.

Another chapter was born,
about a wildlife riddle.

13.

He veered towards the elephants,
to get a result,

Who became furious,
at this blatant insult.

Gerry then turned,
running at the lions full blast,

Who saw a solitary giraffe,
coming at them fast.

14.

They were trying
to separate one giraffe,

Like hyenas,
they wanted a scoff and a laugh.

Rampaging elephants
did suddenly appear,

The lions thought,
"Let's get out of here!"

15.

The giraffes saw this,
and ran away too.

Lucky,
because they didn't have a clue

Of the danger there,
seconds before,

With lions closing in,
like a trapdoor.

16.

All the animals panted,
out of breath.

The giraffes escaped
an untimely death

Gerry alleviated
suffering and pain,

He'd acted bravely,
and used his brain.

MICK THE MONKEY

(London, UK) 14-02-1994

MICK THE MONKEY

1.

Mick the monkey
was a hoot and a ball,

Agile and clever,
he never did fall.

Fully grown,
graceful as could be,

Flying from branch to branch,
tree to tree.

2.

Other monkeys knew
Mick was the best.

On the ground,
he'd do somersaults with zest.

He'd stamp his feet,
holler and shout.

That's what Mick the monkey
was all about.

3.

Life was great,
but hadn't always been so.

As all had to be quiet,
and be in tow

Of Maurice the bully,
who shoved his weight about

Threatening others,
when he'd scream and shout.

4.

He left the group
after something funny,

When he'd blown it
for acting like a dummy.

He got too big
for each monkey boot,

Bellowing and bullying,
when he did hoot.

MICK THE MONKEY

5.

That's the call he used
to take on all comers,

Confidently thinking,
"They'll all be runners."

Mick ignored him,
like smart animals do.

Maurice persisted,
for him it wouldn't do.

6.

Maurice's nose,
was always out of joint,

"Fighting's great," he thought,
"That's the point."

He didn't have
an intelligent existence,

He only had
his dogged persistence.

7.

"Fight me Mick,
or do you scare?

Let's go for it,
if you dare!"

"Maurice,
the day is beautiful and sunny.

Drop this,
let's all do something funny."

8.

"No way!" cried Maurice,
"Let's have a test!

In my heart,
I know I'm best."

"What do you suggest?"
Mick showed all his teeth,

Knowing Maurice,
would come to grief.

9.

"I don't know."
Maurice looked nonplussed,

"I do," said Mick
"You don't mind being rushed?"

"No not at all," said Maurice,
"what's your idea?

Whatever it is,
I've no fear."

10.

"See those branches,
between each tree?

Let's leap from one to the other,
do you agree?

It will test our strength,
and it will do,

To see whose best,
between me and you."

11.

"Okay," said Maurice,
forgetting he was a little fat.

He went first,
and fell to the ground, SPLAT!

Above him,
Mick flew through the air,

Catching overhanging branches,
without a care.

12.

The other monkeys,
hooted and did shout,

Showing their teeth,
in the ritual leap about.

Maurice groaned,
and slinked off saying, "I did fail."

Last thing they saw of him,
was his sad departing tail.

13.

Things then became
really good,

There was even enough
jungle wood.

Later Mick saw
Maurice slinking along,

Who he liked,
even though he'd been wrong.

14.

He said,
"Maurice, come on back to the fold!

We need you,
you're courageous and bold."

Maurice showed his teeth,
for one and all to see,

Happy now,
he swung from a branch on a tree.

15.

All now live together,
in harmony as one.

There's always a lot of laughs,
plenty fun.

It doesn't pay,
to be a bully and bad,

As you'll end up,
alone and sad!

BILLY THE BEE

(London, UK) 4-14-1994

SUNBUDDY FABLES #3

1.

Billy the bee
liked to joke with his pals,

By dive-bombing
to disturb the cows.

Sad for them,
they could only swish a tail,

Attached to their behinds,
next to the milking pail.

2.

Farmer said,
"I've had enough!"

He lumbered off,
with a huff and a puff.

He was furious
with those unruly bees,

"They should leave 'em alone,
and play in the trees."

3.

He had insect repellent,
when he did return.

Billy had a sharp lesson
to learn.

He shut the barn door
and did spray

Above the cows heads,
so no bees got away.

4.

A kindly man,
no living creature did he kill.

Compassion for others,
he did feel.

So the spray was not deadly,
but foul.

It didn't affect humans,
dogs, or a cow.

5.

Any other time,
Billy wouldn't survive the day.

With spray cans, bumble bees
are easy prey.

All inhaled,
coughed, and choked as one,

Suddenly,
life was no longer fun.

6.

The door opened,
all fled gasping for air.

The bees turn blue
for not playing fair.

The winged creatures
made a rasping sound

Before collapsing
onto the ground.

7.

Billy said,
"I don't feel brill.

What I inhaled,
made me ill."

"I'm sick," his mate said,
heaving and groaning.

All around were bees,
whining and moaning.

8.

"Billy," said his mate,
desperation in his voice,

"I can't fly,
and that's not my choice.

All I want to do
is go home.

My day's ruined, it's horrible,
it's blown."

9.

"I know," said Billy,
voice full of fear.

Above him, a normally passive cow
did appear.

He was furious,
from his hoofs to his big wet nose.

Billy thought,
"It's all my fault, so here goes."

10.

"I'm sorry Mr. Cow,
for being a fool.

I thought dive-bombing you
was really cool.

So please,
just stamp on me.

I'm the one to punish,
that's my plea."

11.

"You can't demand,
anything at all.

You're all guilty,"
said the cow so tall.

"But I'll deal with you first,
with my hoof.

There'll be nothing left of you,
no proof."

12.

"So be it," said Billy,
for the very last time.

The sun felt lovely,
in the hot summer clime.

A small tear
appeared from his eye,

He thought,
"Oh well, I had to try."

13.

Bees were buzzing,
what a scene.

Thinking,
"Billy is almost a has-been."

The hoof came down,
with an almighty clump.

They thought Billy
was now a dead lump.

14.

Mooing laughter was heard,
above each head.

Mr. Cow's anger had gone,
this is what he said.

"Little bees on the ground,
every dog has his day.

Making my life a misery,
was a bad game to play."

15.

"Learn this lesson:
Just because I'm meek,

Doesn't mean
I'm totally soft and weak.

Your joke backfired,
it wasn't funny.

Now be off
and make some honey."

16.

They all flew off,
real slow,

Wings clipped
by events of the day's show.

Billy said,
"I'll never again bomb dive.

I know I'm lucky
just to be alive."

BIFFO THE BEAR

(London, UK) 15 - 04 -1994

BIFFO THE BEAR

1.

Biffo the bear
was a fearsome sight,

Crashing through the forest
with awesome might.

Normally,
he was in a good frame of mind.

On a quest now
for something he must find.

2.

Honey,
was what it was all about.

He was angry,
so he gave a tree a clout.

Tree shuddered,
with shock and pain.

As Biffo looked,
for sweet tasting gain.

3.

"I'm starving!" he yelled,
into the Canadian wood.

The birds flew off,
because they could.

"My taste buds
are doing somersaults inside!

I'm a bear,
selfish feelings I don't hide."

4.

He was in
a disgusting frame of mind,

His rage
had made him blind.

Others stood
well clear.

Biff on the rampage,
something to fear.

5.

He roared,
showing his teeth,

Gnashing them together,
getting no relief.

"When I get honey,
I'll scrag the home of the bee.

As they've tried to conceal it
from me."

6.

He hit
all the trees in his path.

He was a million miles away
from a laugh.

Then he saw a bee,
buzzing and alive,

Thinking,
"He'll lead me to his hive."

7.

The bee flew onwards,
and then did disappear.

Biff knew the honey
was very near.

Arriving at the hive,
he did bellow and shout.

Then smelt the honey
by raising his snout.

8.

The bees knew
they were in big trouble.

They flapped their wings,
at the double.

Didn't faze Biff,
not in the least,

He was after all,
a woodland beast.

9.

They tried to sting him,
to no avail.

It was obvious
he would prevail.

Problem was,
he intended to wreck the hive,

So the queen bee
wouldn't survive.

10.

For a bee,
that's the very worst.

As the colony's unity
would burst.

Biffo gorged,
over and over again,

Which created,
an awful stomach pain.

11.

This took him
completely by surprise.

So painful,
he couldn't rise.

He whined,
for any to listen at all,

Seeming to shrivel
and go small.

12.

"Their no sympathy for me,
in this plight.

All must agree,
I'm a sorry sight."

"Serves you right,"
said a squirrel on the ground.

He had skipped up,
hardly made a sound.

13.

"Don't even waste
your air!

Whatever you think,
I don't care."

Biff felt awful,
and was out of his mind,

He just wanted
others to be kind.

14.

"A lesson in gluttony,
can come to us all.

Whether small like you,
or big and tall.

It's funny," he said,
"How life balances out.

I acted
like a mindless soccer lout."

15.

"You get it now,"
the squirrel nuzzled his ear.

"Just stop destroying things,
is that clear?"

"Yeah," said Biff,
"That's the way it's got to be.

It took a stomach ache,
for my eyes to see."

SHEILA THE SKUNK

(London, UK) 18-4-1994

SUNBUDDY FABLES #3

1.

Sheila the skunk
had a heart of gold.

Meek and mild,
opposite of bold.

She had a problem
that wouldn't abate.

Causing her grief,
and affecting her fate.

2.

One day she realised,
something wasn't normal.

Skunks around her
started becoming formal.

They acted
like something wasn't right,

As she endured
their malice and spite.

SHEILA THE SKUNK

3.

"Something's wrong,
its not the same.

Nothing been said,
no one's to blame.

Still, I need to know
what to do,

As I haven't
a clue."

4.

She went for advice
and a sound word.

Seeing the wise owl,
the big white bird.

It was a distance,
where he resided,

To the tall tree,
from where he glided.

5.

Sheila thought,
"Maybe he doesn't know."

Wondering,
if she should go.

Her faith returned,
as she neared her destination,

Seeing the wise owl
in deep contemplation.

6.

She approached,
feeling silly and shy.

She lost it,
and begun to cry.

He flew down,
"What's the problem my dear?

The worst is over,
you've nothing to fear."

SHEILA THE SKUNK

7.

His voice
had a soothing calming sound,

Maybe a solution
really could be found.

She explained
what happened that day,

How male skunks
just turned away.

8.

He listened,
then glazed over in his eyes,

Oblivious,
to the buzzing flies.

The silence seemed
to go on forever,

But he was wise,
and ever so clever.

SUNBUDDY FABLES #3

9.

He said,
"My mind's totally blank.

I don't know,
if I'm honest and frank."

She left wishing,
she hadn't bothered to go.

Such a depressing answer,
a terrible blow.

10.

Dejected,
she reeled from side to side,

Feeling worthless,
with no pride.

Confused about what
to do for the best,

Pushed over her limits,
a painful test.

11.

That night she slept
tail over her face,

Trying to find
a peaceful place.

She felt the owl
drop down from flight,

Renowned for being,
as 'Silent As The Night.'

12.

He said,
"I've found what's disturbed your calm.

What's causing
your sadness and harm.

None would say,
it's not their place,

Not wanting you
to lose face."

13.

"You've eaten food
sprayed with insecticide.

Others feel let down,
it's damaged their pride.

It was no good,
totally unclean.

Mind you,
they have been mean."

14.

"It also changed
your skunky smell -

Not an easy thing
for others to tell.

This info,
is for your heart.

You need
a fresh start."

15.

"Thank you,
I could break out into song!

I knew they thought
I was wrong.

It makes sense,
eating as natural as can be,

They were a little cruel,
but I totally agree."

16.

She avoided sprayed food,
man made styles,

Supplementing her diet
with feminine wiles.

She had no problem
finding a mate,

Life did a full circle,
becoming great.

THE END